ACES

George McCauley

SOMETHING MORE PUBLICATIONS

Something More Publications
2504 Belmont Ave.
Bronx, N.Y. 10458

ISBN 0-9622889-2-6

Library of Congress Catalogue Card Number: 91-90578
Printed in the United States of America

The publication of this book is supported by a grant from the George Link, Jr. Foundation, Inc.

For Bernie, Vera and The Cast

Contents

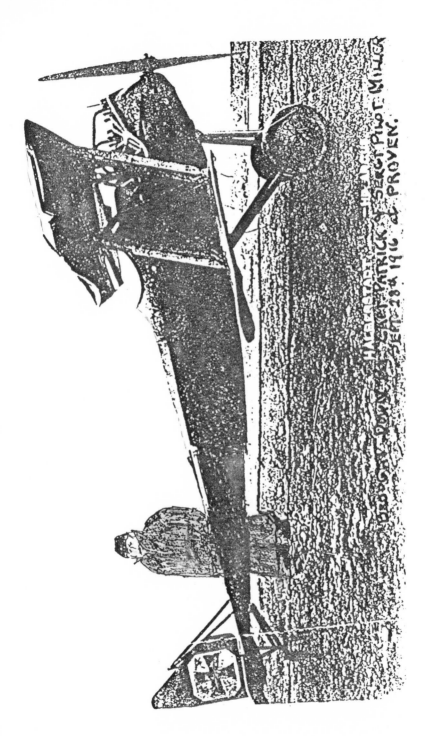

HALBERSTADT — THE SHIP PATRICK & SGT. PILOT F. MILLER DROVE DOWN SEPT. 28TH 1916 at PROVEN.

ACES

I

He knows a window opens
on as wide a world as
heart has beat against
in fear or yearning. A
taste for wilderness, he
calls it, a striding
spirit, like the cock out-
side his hut who marches
up and down beneath neg-
lected flowers trailing
from his window sill—its
nature is to crow more
largely than itself. 'You
live', he offers to the
beam above his cot, 'as
far as you will venture
forth to die.'

This matins said, he rocks
his morning body smoothly
to its feet and shuffles
out to splash cold water
from the make-shift pipe.
Barn-smells, sharp and
cloying, rise around him,
scent his towel; he almost
feels for haystalks in his
hair. He whistles off his
beard to Annie Laurie, is
bemused by what he sees
in the uncertain mirror,
suddenly thinks of biscuits,
bacon, bracing tea, pre-
fering these to what he
doesn't understand.

II

The sun is slow to answer
reveille. It hunches in the
east behind the haunting mists
that creep from nearby woods.
He dresses in its russet glow,
his body welcoming successive
layers of sheep's wool, cowhide,
goat, their skins becoming
his, the warmth, the treated
smell, the memory of the hunt—
that strange embrace of man
and animal from old.

His jaunty scarf belies its
humble purpose: keep the cold
from tearing at his heart,
protect his face from the
unseemly flames that sometimes
search about his cockpit.
Gloves, more pat and paw than
grip, he throws into the helmet
waiting upside down on his cot,
its ears relaxed, its goggles
empty-eyed, not even a life-
less stare. No gaudy amulet
or magic plume to cap his
complicated harness; only
disbelievers worry about fate.
He worries cheerfully how
he looks.

III

The daily ritual begins. A
mission. We go in at oh six
hundred hours. Are there any
questions?

Measured how, he wonders.
From a starbirth? From the
intimidating headstart of
the sun's rays? From the
first crack of earth's crust?
From the primitive moon roll-
ing onto the night sky like
a silver dollar in a poker
game? From Abraham's call?

Now *there's* a perfect back-
drop for a war!—the headlong
exodus, a land grab; my
advantage, checkmate; sudden
switch—your move, I lose. No
motives what they seem, no end
in sight. And then it's over.
Yahweh made a deal.

His memory is spotty but sup-
ports his reservations: Caleb
faking estimates of enemy
defenses, patriotic Judith
talking everyone, including
God, to death; the brawler,
Samson, losing his edge; the
time that Saul was sitting
on the potty, David wouldn't

shoot him; priests like chid-
ing air-raid wardens; prophets
sliding down the intervening
centuries like firemen on
poles; the thin-lipped mother
of the Macabees with her
expensive views on politics;
the magi scrounging up a map;

Salome twirling her tote bag.

IV

Then the new breed, Jesus.
Guarantees you'll beat the
body count. His squadron motto:
'generated, never made'. He
never made it either, crashed
in flames of love and innocence.
They found a wooden model of
a church, half-carved, beneath
his cot, along with regulation
parachute and letters home he
never mailed.

There was some talk of sight-
ings, raucous singing in the air,
a perfumed scarf identified as
his, the usual ghost plane stuff.

V

Why add to anybody's martyr-
ology? His own prefered
solution was old-fashioned:
slap their face and walk away.
Impractical, of course. The
din of faces slapped would rise,
as thick as flak, from dressing
rooms, accounting houses, rail-
road stations, picnic grounds,
infirmaries, from every store
or tavern, chapel, office,
orphanage or seaside carnival
that ever was.

When people suffer more from
what they can't than what they
can, the whining can get
deafening.

That's why he flies.

VI

Is there a human altitude,
he asks, I mean that suits
our wingless frame? This day,
he's told to top at several
hundred metres. High is
relative. He's seen the condor
bank indifferently above his
battle, heard woodsmen chop-
ping far up cliffs he hugged
below for cover, pulled his
stick into his groin to miss
an oak tree angled like a
screech in his path, dived
down sheer ravines, escaping
his pursuers who were still
debating high and low when
they hit ground hard. You
have to factor wind and weight,
the bloated smell of gasoline,
a presence at your back, a
puzzling sameness occupying
the horizon, clouds tinting
imperceptibly, an instinct for
what isn't there, one comrade's
uncertainty, smugness in an-
other's airborne carriage—
some formula distilled from
all of these that makes you
reach suddenly up for more sky
and more. No insolence intend-
ed, no regret conceded.

And yet it's tempting to remain
above it all. He's watched
them scurry down below, heads

12

carried to and fro on legs,
the mudfolk, how they dig
dark holes called homes, mark
off, in puffs of tangled
steel, the bounds of their
imaginary safety, spy on one
another's strengths, forage
for pathetic comforts, caress
their weapons late at night,
put off their friends with
facile nicknames, void them-
selves in secret, endure the
ambient stench, take out the
anger of their deprivations
on all comers, plot sensuous
retreats, give random birth
to strangers out of strangers,
lodge their demands at passing
shrines: madonnas with over-
wrought bosoms, cherubs in
diapers, mustachioed saints.

It's not the pain that craters
human beings down there, it's
the illusion of it. True pain
has skill to it, refinement.
Unless he finds a way to say
'It's *I* who hurts, it's I,'
unless the fight's *that* close,
a war's just staged hostility.
He'd rather die, his head a
ball of flames, his hair
haloed in fire, his life's
breath sucked into his howling
slipstream, than live that way.

14

VII

The briefing done, he joins
his brothers in hedgehopping
banter, to disguise the nerv-
ousness. Their voices bank
and loop and roll in friendly
competition, each one noticing
the windsock of the other's
mood, their lift and yaw, the
drag allowed in conversation
short of stalling. Topics
have no consequence: revivals
of some past adventure, proper
use of mason jar at higher
altitudes to take a pee, their
favorite enemies, a book they
read on fishing lures, how
bluster often wins promotion.
Menace goes unnamed.

He never wanted more than now
to listen to the softness of
a woman's voice, to have his
words absorbed in her, dis-
charged of all self-doubt and
all bravado, even his silence
heard.

VIII

For all the camaraderie, they
walk out toward their ships
alone. He genuflects to his
(her name is Simple Sam), en-
circles her with practised eye,
a flick of incense to each bolt
and strut and truss, deep bows
at fin and rudder, anoints her
fuselage where scars appear—
fatigue, devotion, blooding—
traces with his reverential fing-
ertip the camber of her breasted
wings.

Metaphors end at her Gorgon head:
what shape is the propellor in?
It rules his rhythms, *is* him
in a sense—his thrust, restraint
when called upon, his apoplectic
speed, his measured shudder at
the kill.

It comes to him again: he only
stewards power; all else rides
on this machine that bucks and
hurtles through impassive space
like earth itself with people
clinging to its sides in wonder.

IX

That's why the gesture seems
incongruous: mechanics hold-
ing out a parachute for him
like dainty underthings; soft
silk and hope you never have
to wave them out of doors.
It's not the implied danger
that upsets him, it's proced-
ure: shroud lines free of
blasted buckles, ripcord sepa-
rate from pencil strung from
stupid clipboard on his chest.

'Parasols belong on boardwalks,'
he persists. The antiquated
sergeant doesn't argue, stuffs
him deftly in his seat, belays
the straps, adjusts the cowling
aft and, with an unction proper
to a sergeant's rank, mumbles
the Almighty in his ear.

X

A cough, like someone in an
empty church, a repetitious
clearing of the throat in the
next room, a staccato hum, in-
decisive like soccer fans in a
tight match, stronger as their
team prevails, one rising note
sustained, convulsed like a
baby's hapless protest, then
a settled drone, muscular, his
motor comes to life.

His taxi takes him down a barely
level field. Gray flowers bend
their faces from his churning
dust. He bumps around the
farthest fringe of trees and
turns his craft into a wind
that jolts his teeth, contests
his progress every inch of
runway, till he lifts at last,
light and free, slowly to mount
the day.

It's only then that he acknow-
ledges the presence of this
stranger in his plane, the gun,
lined up with his very being
as if to channel all his canny
senses into one: the pressure
of his finger on its crescent
trigger. People say he's good
at it.

He is embarrassed by compar-
isons with sport and art and
virtuosity of other kinds.
He knows a demon when he sees
one, this swarthy, phallic,
adamantine gun with manic eyes
and leaden drool, that stands
like a forbidding angel at the
gate of his elusive paradise
where all he wants to do is
fly, to join the dance—with
friend or foe it's all the same
to him—to match his steps
against the best, to whirl and
lock, to soar and light with
style. Instead, he kills what
he would imitate, despoils
what he admires most. He al-
most sobs, 'Can joy be wrenched
from all this butchery?'

XII

The mission proves routine.
An enemy dissolves in orange
in his gunsight, another falls
away in a glissade, like some-
one dropping from a building
top who tries to right himself
before he hits. At least that
dignity. A friend gets over-
confident and pays. A doe-eyed
novice leaves formation and sur-
vives. The planes seem strange-
ly squat to him, snub-nosed and
rickety as they round and round
on one another.

It's afterwards, when danger's
past and thumbs are raised in
mutual salute, he feels a
desperate weight inside his
chest, a truth as bleak and
frowning as a windless world,
a confession, if you will: for
his kind, there is no base to
return to.

XIII

And when, one day, death meets
him in the sky, locks on his
tail, when his great art is
spent, his gentle grip brings
no response, his matchless eye
is veiled, his housing folded
in on him, his guages running
down,

when clouds are pillowed so
far up he cannot limp away
to hide, when in his wind-
screen he beholds a shattered
sun, when the riddle's finally
done,

then he remembers Jesus and a
song they used to sing into
the smoke at the canteen, trac-
ing its notes with beer mugs
raised, conducting, with their
eye-brows, loud and soft parts
for the rowdy chorus of young
hopes around them:

>Blessed are the ones
>who fly. They'll be
>in heaven long before
>they die.

MARQUETRY

MESSENGER

"Then Mary brought a pound
of very costly perfume, pure
oil of nard, and anointed
the feet of Jesus and wiped
them with her hair." (Jn 12:3)

His body lengthens on the
pillowed seat, his shoulders
pivot limply, chin craning
imperceptibly, his garlic
breath runs harder now
down to where the lush hair
arcs from her prostrate
form, seeks him, folds and
folds around his feet adrip
with her smothering perfum-
ed jelly, captures his pale
ankles in its puffed black
swirl, flicks at his legs,
channels between his toes,
catches into little wisps
on his rough nails, pushes
into his pores, draws forth
his vagabond smell, absorb-
ing all, rubs his skin to
purple ivory. Not bad for
a preacher man who's on his
feet a lot. She seems to
like it, too.

TOO LONG AT SCHOOL

I watch the line kick out in step,
gray, ivied thoughts in better
time than tune; for all the frothy
pep they generate, their thin-lipped
mime seems somewhat winded, short
on joy; but for them it's the real McCoy.

Center-stage a figure stands behind
his unlit pipe; he holds great slabs
of history in his hands like a deck
of cards and folds the Joker under.
'Pick any one', he coaxes, 'just for fun'.

A lady dances from the wings with
loveless, labored grace, intent upon
the one-note song she sings about her
famous predicament: how to get what
men have gotten without seeming
just as rotten.

Another presses flowers, pins them on
an orange sun sprinkled with mango seeds;
her paper fins fan out, she dips into
a wrinkled curtsy. Masquerade or revel,
is this really graduate level?

'Look deep into my extra eye', he says,
'the one up near my brain; it calculates
to the square of pi the distance from
pleasure and pain'. Its lens is slightly
elongated so feelings don't get overstated.

A gaunt man strokes a student's cheek
and stares into a mirror. 'Oh, how
innocent, how shy and weak this child;
he's doomed to live below the level he
could really be. I mean, the lad is
so much me'.

Her forte is the after-id, a variation
on a tic induced from overstriding as
a kid in soggy underpants. 'We pick
our poisons', scream the audience,
but she insists she makes good sense.

The gloves and hat, an engineer's,
the overalls, a stoker's by their look;
the last among his peers you'd take for
teaching poli-sci. He needs the cover from
the chalk that billows out above his talk.

His collar says, Divine — reading
theology. A pantheon of stone-eyed
prelates seem to ring him round, their
mitred gaze descending on a Liliputian
Christ crouched down before their
unforeshortened frown.

A beard curls down a stack of books.
Its owner on the other side sits
scribbling with a will. He looks up,
fiercely overcome with pride. 'I've
found the very thing I swore will
save us from discovering more'.

SHOOTOUT

Your turned-down
face contorted,
fluted brow, skull
solidly behind it
all the way, nostrils
nearly at a shout,
eyes busy net-
working, cheeks like
someone chewing
something, lips mid-
quiver, teeth at the
ready, pedestal chin.

No trace, I'd have
to say, of subtle
sentiment or inter-
rupted joy.

It seems that you
don't like me
writing poetry.

Which is it?

BESTIARY

Do we own the world
with our eyes? Or
does it hypnotize us
like the *cat* craning
at some elusive hum,
or splayed in rigid
adoration at the hollow
space where last it
saw a morsel, *mouse*?

Do we clock time, ad-
justing days and years
to some internal chime
that tames the fears?
Or are we rightly driven
forth from here like
the *bird* that finds
no other reason for its
wise design than to fly?

Can we kill, content
with our justifications,
spill blood that doesn't
lie in basins somewhere
we can drill for it? Or,
like the *lion*, do we
simply relish meat and
suffer no distraction
from our grinding purpose,
need the sweaty work-out,
savor scented remnants
dripping from our chins?

Do we love God? Do angels
entertain us, hasten with
their rod to strike the
firmament and bring us rain?
Do saints wave palms in our
train? Or, like the *bat*,
do we dangle upside down
by day, heads filled with
blood, and streak by
night in eyeless flight,
our frantic hearts just
hoping for the homing?

CHILDWORLD

Not street where people live, you
fool, but where we played, a sacred
space, our space, buttoned with man-
hole covers, an arena with no audi-
ence save us, a wonder world of curbs
and tar, of cobbled stones and rail-
ings, any ledge that gave a handhold,
uncomplaining walls to lean on,
overhangs against the rain, tree
limbs maybe you could reach that fed
like veins to other trees or, better,
roofs (a subject in itself), doorways
full of secrets, splintered poles'
to dare the climber, stoops to wait
and wait on, hedges where you dis-
appeared at will, lamp-posts for your
aim, windows to worry you, alleys
ending in adventure, with some luck
a plot of dirt that generated mud
and worms and pebbles, gracefully
took the point of a knife, drain-
pipes that carried messages, anything
crenellated, places you could start
an echo, endless shortcuts, any
elevation for a lookout, cars with
runningboards and chariot wheels,
trickling water that led to the sea,
the least incline defeating gravity,
hydrants hard as a bull's head,
stanchions anchoring your games,

coal-chutes into darkness, pavement
squares you'd designate a million
ways, whatever served as boundary-
line or forbidden goal, fences to
clamber and dogs to avoid, sewers
that swallowed impassively the good
with the bad, gratings to fish in,
a familiar, constant sky shaped by
the building tops. All this and
nothingness beyond. Street, you
jackass. We're not talking inter-
personal relationships. Can
someone help me translate this?

THE MAN WITH NO UNCONSCIOUS

He puts his teeth in in the
morning one at a time, never
confuses them with pocket
change or his toenails. A
bellows in his head lets
air in and out. Up to noon
he eats one corn flake,
moistened first, dresses his
children in wicker-work.

That's his wife in the drive-
way laughing at his nose.
This puzzles him. He gath-
ers who he is from advertise-
ments, leaves his image be-
hind in mirrors, thinks
outrageous is a place.
Everyone titters now: from
the side he looks like
plywood.

He's seldom drawn to horses'
sheen, hair on flowers, rain
slicks, hollow trees or
garden pools that swallow
the sun. With his melting
radials, you'd think he'd
stick to walls, rub off on
bannisters and that, but he
moves right along. Even on
his best day, he'd never
call God interesting.

APOCALYPSE AGAIN

Desert Storm, 1991

On Land ...

I've seen the worm beside me
squished, another floating up-
side down in spittle. (You get
to know which side is up or
down). We worms make friends
with dirt; slime seems like
Waikiki to us. Life underfoot
is not the terror you might
think. Each day is progress.

I'd stretch a point to say I
wouldn't like, at times, to be
a periscope, or cover ground at
higher speeds. And those who
try to meet my needs can never
seem to find the right end to
begin on. I dislike most of all
—when someone makes me bait—
why do they also use a lure?

On Sea ...

My aunt was heavy, even for a
hippopotamus, but full of wise
advice. She said to plant my
slit eyes on the water's rim,
two feet or so behind my nos-
trils. That really scares them.
Not to mention my devastating
clod-hoppers, imposing shoulder
pads and a jaw like a fork-lift.

43

Below the waist, I taper like
a body-builder, and yet total
strangers use me for a flight
deck, flamingos, gulls and, once,
a crocodile. Flies whisper
innuendos in my ear at night.
I cannot clean my bum, consult
a dermatologist or do aerobics.
Why can't I just swim like others
in my habitat?

And In The Air . . .

Space has no sides, the eagle
gliding there complains. I
cannot rest at either end.
And though I've never pulled
thread through needle, met
the rent, or eaten bulrush,
I'm supposed to be bald truth
and sentinel and noble pre-
dator rolled into one.

I have feathers for a heart,
talons I don't know what to
do with when I fly, a medi-
terranean nose, and diffi-
culty swallowing food off the
shelf. I land feet first, and
sometimes cannot fit through
doorways. Why does wingspan
make a person great?

*

America, America, God holds you
on a leash. Unless you recog-
nize the beast in you, he'll cut
your popcorn off and feed you to
the big computer. You'll have
to think successively. He'll
bury you in junk mail; all your
knightly kit will rust. Because
your favorite sport is television
wrestling, He will make you
stumble over bottle caps and
strangle on your yellow ribbons.

This God chases justice like the
hyperactive waterbug, plows after
mercy like the ox in harness,
has long since found a better way
to say it than a burning bush.
His name is Peace, and we are
His menagerie.

HOT AND COLD

Christmas, 1990

No poem this year for Christmas?
World so empty, winter in the soul,
no urge to raise a knuckled glass
around the blazing nutmeg bowl,

my thoughts congealed like steaming blocks
of ice, my confidence a crack-
ing pond, rimed whiskers on the clock's
face at night, a rutted track

across my glacier heart, the mem-
ories of flowered summer love
reduced to pungent mulch, a sem-
blance of a sun nailed above,

hopes snow-blind, my secret fear
of snapping like distended trees,
desire pawing like a deer
in deep snow, a total freeze,

nor noise to match the tumult in
the womb where Mary, lovely pale,
makes him merry, a mandolin
on her comely knee. Why no wassail?

*

A child stands timid sentinel,
its gaunt eyes two receding cones;
its mother, stippled by a shell
blast, bleeds into the pavement stones.

A father hates, his sons concur;
they memorize the tribal foes,
the ancient hurt, the recent slur,
the superstitions—on it goes.

46

A playroom strewn with children, 'his'
and 'hers' and 'ours'; one sullen boy
belies this cordial emphasis;
he twists the head off a startled toy.

They tell me of salons, quite drawn,
with scented music piped through walls
running with mascara scenes of dawn
and bursting wheat and waterfalls,

for ladies only, sitting in smocks,
regrets unseemly, courage best;
as each one tosses back her locks,
a mighty suction does the rest.

And then the woman *I* am, big
with image, buxom mother-muse,
who feeds me like a ravished pig,
but just as quickly might refuse

me feelings, fancies, aching words;
a sorceress, a bitch, her store
of magic shuttered and my bird's
beak hanging. What is birthing for?

*

But even Scrooge's ghosts move on.
Let's say this passing chill was due
to sweetbreads spiced with tarragon
or too much grog shared by a few

too few. I'm minded that each time
we celebrate this feast is grace,
that no one gets the paradigm
or calculates the leap in space

47

that Jesus takes so lightly save
those gifted by the Holy Ghost,
who hastens from its polar cave
to make our spectral hearts its boast.

Ah, then the crackling! Sky like chalk
blue panes, an air so rarified
each object, like a sharpened stalk,
startles the eye. Against a wide

horizon, great snow-cathedrals
shoulder upwards, rise atop
primeval piers, with saddle cols
for butresses, a thick outcrop

of cornices, each with seraphs' eyes,
and columns like twisting seracs, tur-
bans on their heads; and music flies
up couloirs climbing from the fir

tree floor below like organ pipes,
deep crevasses cut aisles between
grotesque ice-figures, different types
of angel carvings rarely seen,

and gold and purple crystals grow
to rounded windows, quiet suns
veined with immortal mistletoe,
and joyous, wrenching glory runs
down like an avalanche.

*

It's up
to us then, friends, to find some soar-
ing reason to adorn our cup
this happy Christmas and ignore

the frost-bite. For, all temperatures
belong to God, who doesn't shun
the lower registers, endures,
at very most, what we have done

to make Him warm and flannel-lined
like a teapot cosy. Evidence
can trickle from a weaker mind
for the other view: that our first sense

is wakened in the womb, a hot
environment to say the least,
and that's the reason like as not
that we light candles at a feast.

It's true that Jesus waited curled,
an incandescent ember, set
to breathe his fire on the world
and melt its mood. But we forget

that Mary was a troubador;
she knew the lyrics must be bold—
a poet's more secure when more
exposed. So, here's to Christ born cold!

END MAN

The book of Job describes a passing incident,
no more. The man recovered. That's why I refuse
to sit among your ashes like an occupant,
endlessly pick your scabs, effuse
about how glad I am to certify your brief,
listen to your sour, repetitious grief.

Job's problems had no ordinary source. His name,
in fact, decoded from that ancient tongue, can mean,
'where is my father?' or, with more edge to the game,
'where is the one who hates me?' Men are ever keen
to probe their fragile origin in God, to find
out if His wizened grip is safe, His rutting blind.

So Job attacks as much as ever he was set
upon by Father-God. He slues about, squirts bile
on altars. His living death-mask snaps at God's net
with its teeth, demanding to consult his file.
He noses into whirlwinds, lets fly disfigured screams,
his silhouette a claw against the sky. Sick dreams.

Job's therapists consult some other manual.
They deal in arguments, like lawyers, move the chess
men up and down the board, are ruled by communal
propriety, explain away the loneliness
of pain, take note of God's great size and fickle ways.
'When God hurls thunderbolts, the just man ducks and prays.'

Alright for business, I suppose, but don't they
miss Job's fun! It's overacting that achieves
release. Job trusts enough, is trusted, to display
his feelings vaudeville style. That God plays end man peeves
his would-be healers. All the potions they devise
are meant to rob God of His greatest gift, surprise.

So, leave your dunghill, friend, if you can't take
on God. Farm out your pain to lesser agencies
who'd never dare impute an absolute mistake
on high and hand out pale, addictive remedies.
Job's fame hangs on the way his story grew.
Each time he'd give the grim details, he'd add a few.

MARKET STREET

... for several instruments

A busy San Francisco
                              sky. The burly
clouds climb on
                         up Powell from Market,
winded westward
                         to where people live
in houses, and then to
                         the sea. I find my dying
here, if these indeed be me
                         who scratch at flinty
sidewalks for their life's
                         blood, hope their way
through garbage
                         cans, grip their chest
hair against an evil
                         wind from the Bay.

This part
                    the copper-colored people,
dry as desert,
                              same dirty
beard on most, disinviting
                              your glance;
the giveaway's the smell,
                              a parody
on sweet, a vintage
                         presence. Leather
jackets chafed
                         chalk-white,
held on with wire, string,
                         anything, bed-rolls
slung like powder horns,
                              shoulders

clenched, the pointy
                    boots always a better
cut than you'd expect.

The scurry, zigzag,
                    hustle, a higher version
of the durable
                    pigeons that poke
at curious crumbs,
                    reconnoiter sticky
cartons, gaping cups,
                    cigar butts, test all
spirits. Some fall
                    in step, you think
with you, make their
                    play in a faint croak
or clipped
                    demand, a reverential
wheeze, wheel off
                    when it fails, go
find one of their own
                    to gesticulate
about their bad luck.
                    Some seem unhinged,
their eyebrows almost
                    circular; they subtly
urge you turn
                    them down so they can hate
more, rub
                    your nose in their forlorn
reality.

53

One mama sits

                        discomfitted, her

thighs so visited by men

                               or more,

she's learned

                    the art of finishing

one conversation with

                      successive partners;

you hear her broadcast

                      now from her marble

spot by the BART,

                a high-pitched monotone

into the swirl of eyeless

                    commuters passing

her hell-bent.

                    They pick up only

snatches of her pain,

                       how she fronts

best she can her

                       ravaged, still

raging dignity.

An ominous young

                    man, strung-out on

something, dangles sandled

                  feet from the island

stop where flat-faced

                    trollies coast by.

Folks waiting

                  for the 7 look away

from his spittle and

                  sing-song screech,

wonder if he'll lose

                  his leggings. His

skinny-elbowed

                girl friend rouses

him in time, but only

                  to an ecstacy

of beating on the trolley's

               side and tearing at

its riggings like a buccaneer

                   his booty.

Some dumb Wisconsin

           licence rolls his window

down, gets punched in

            his snooping Japanese

camera for his troubles,

             like Uncle Clarence

warned him twice and will

             doubtlessly rehearse

the entire bitter

              winter in De Pere.

Across the street a

              plump man eyes

the smallest print

               on glaring

porno posters.

             Into specialties.

He's come to town

            to see a pimple

on a rounded woman's

           breast, an urge he gets

in the sun-scorched

           emptiness east of here

where he almost lives;

                    it grows into a groaning
until he hiccups all
                    the time, then dons
those red suspenders
                                peeking out
beneath his worsted suit.

Farther south the Civic
                                Center curves
off Market like
                                the serious
end of a tomahawk,
                    great squares of squat
stone, state and federal
                                caliphates, ample
fire-fields to
                    solace any lover of the
arts who'd brave
                    the night for Don Giovanni.
The whole is entered past
                    a dried up fountain
where some winos, wedged
                    among its massive water
figures, suck
                                their crumpled
bags of Thunderbird and Wild
                                Irish Rose, argue
in their heads with vanished
                    fathers, children, life
itself, or, when
                    it hurts too much,
blink the grinning
                                curtain down.

No tremor

                in the earth to match

these scenes, no

                shudder to make

you quake more, pangs

                but no bright

birth here. So much

                for Lady Poverty.

Yet, down toward Embarcadero

                where Market starts

to swagger, spruces up,

                where traders walk on stilts

and smart women snap

                their long skirts to the

click of their businesslike

                heels, where posher

tourists drill

                the doorman and the taxi

driver for the lowdown,

a solitary figure, black

                —you bet!

leans back against

                an eerie pastel

fence that masks

                debris from new

construction underway.

He lifts, lofts

                       a soulful

clarinet, mutes

           his pain for this moment

of beauty, spools

                    his healing

music upward, playing

                    for no one,

gone inside

                 himself for good,

for the living God,

             who has to come

out soft and strong just

            like his cry, his song,

to be true in this

              wilderness. His

fingernails caress each

           key, his neck veins

blue on ebony,

         he gives out everything

he has, not

             for money, not

for you or me, but

            for the music.

AFRICAN INTERLUDE

PRELUDE

The wind warps trees,
slants even sky;
its sultry moan is carried
on the whipping vines.
Blossoms like megaphones.

Is there a message
more than rain
in these leaves lapping,
this luxuriant shiver?
The lizards, flattened
to the bark like lice
in swaying dreadlocks,
do not answer.

GROWING PAINS

Pretty girl, your carnival smile undoes
me. Tiny fingers like antennae
scan the rough pew in front as
you calibrate His presence. Gray
rivers of tepid milk for eyes,
yet you grope for the mystery,
accept its rules. Are you so wise
you'd even expect angels? You see
but darkly my misshapen form,
listen instead with your whole
bony being for God's light, warm
to Him who scarified your soul,
like you two had a secret thing
going—your simple dress askew,
He aflame this Pentecost. You sing
me sadness all the same. So few
years calendered for innocence
like yours, so hard to side-step spears
less aimed than His. Will you still dance
when the great darkness nears?

CHOIR LOFT

The melodies are imports mostly,
with familiar plots: sweet
somebody or other, gilded patrons,
undocumented angels, anorexic
hopes, a deity that's uttered in
such tortured grammar as to keep
its mystery intact.

They resonate of blessed river-
banks and battlefields, of goods
in shortage and a famine of time,
of parlous choices and voluptuous
content. A reworked mix of Empire
and Kingdom. Standard stuff.

But something else intrudes. A
beat, hands and feet off the
expected line of song, like
scrambled sonar, a rhythmic clap,
soft toe-tap, a show of heel.
Elbows, shoulders pulsate in a
third direction still.

The multifactored beat restores,
gives body, blood to tired drone.
It sweeps into my soul to play
against my tempo, tunes me
differently.

Thonx be to the Load Goad, I
learn! So much for iambs, dis-
appointed trochees, anapests in
a rout. The thing to ask about
a poem is: can you dance to it?

THE SHOOTING GROUNDS

Andrew Jonah preaching from the iron
van. Attending: Army, Mobile Police
and, with a certain sour congruence,
someone from Sanitation. The grid of
bars that press against his face marks
Andrew's tribe: armed robbers. Now
he's just a man in chains about to die.

The limping catechist, bull neck and
chested, works the makeshift congre-
gation first. Their rifles lounge on
the rutted ground, almost forgotten
as they listen sideways to his story of two
thieves on Calvary—or was it three?—
stealing kingdoms. He's seen a thou-
sand men and women to this exit, so
they know he knows, and honor him
by finishing his sentences.

Then Andrew Jonah speaks, his keel-
like voice ploughing deep troughs,
no nonsense to its timbre, meaning
without masks, straight on conviction
that he's not alone, he is befriended.
Says he got deflected on his way—
like Jonah, got a second chance.
No talk of paying for the past, no
compromise with justice of that bug-
eyed sort. Christ payed it all.
There's nothing for it now but grat-
itude and love—enough, with all his
heart, to make his executioners his
brothers.

The hill across is green with tufting
brush and scrawny, flattop trees.
A pair of temporary flagpoles, much
too tall, bestride the barricade at
either end, their faded crimson canvas
lifted lightly by the slow-moving wind.
We walk with Andrew to the stake, his
outsized shackles clicking off the
distance. Hand in mine, we share the
rituals confusedly, invest each second
with our faith in life, lock eyes to
make the improbable point: there are
no strangers here.

The shooters funnel from the bush,
quick march beneath their flapping
kepis, take their mark. The dignitar-
ies present send a delegate who reads
aloud their version of this sad af-
fair. The catechist warns Andrew
Jonah darkly not to speak again, and
we withdraw. The clumsy business
runs its course, like the oppressive
sun above. Before the end, I prayed
(or did I shout?), "Look, Andrew,
look! Beyond the guns—his peacock
feathers fanned!"

BIG DEAL

The leaders here are thick
from back to front and wide
across, not just the torso
but preeminently the noble
head. Why density should be
conclusive is not clear. It
probably goes back in history:
a spear will pass through
thinner men with more effect;
a hunter sleeps more safely in
a beobad tree than in a bush;
a bulky man's less likely to
neglect his many wives or
they to feed him sparingly.

In my land loud assurance
counts. A man must be cock-
sure on every issue (what's
the history there?). You
claim a space and either edge
opponents off the mat with
pressure at their weakest
point of order, or you throw
them with the quickness of
your tongue.

The leaders here, being padded
like casaba sacks, are free to
seem confused without the risk
of losing ground, because there's
more of them than of the ground.
They save the booming volume
for an enemy or other ceremon-
ial affairs, but spare the
person sitting next to them.

BACKTIME

More like God?
this thunder
shaking stomp, this
tempestuous native
romp? than my ramrod,
perfectly fulcrumed
thought? the knifing
accuracy of my mind,
its high-tech edges
quarrying each
marble slice of world
in bloodless
worded beauty?

Need I navigate
the fire fierce-eyed,
huff my shoulder
feathers, bob sweating
breasts, rotate
my rear-end like
a sprung clockworks
to know something
they know
and I forgot?

DIPLOMACY

My village, I explain, has many pots
(I'm thinking East Side upper 80's
or the 50's around 9th). Well, no,
it can't be reached by auto (on a
weekend maybe, if the Mets are out
of town), but many taxis find a way
(right over you).

The huts are big and cost you many
coconuts (unless they're in the
Bronx or rent-controlled), and each
man knows the other's name (hey, Mac,
get off the schneid!).

Best not to drink too deeply from
its rivers (skip your one and only
chance to walk on water), nor does
fishing in them always pay (the fish
are mutants).

Elders (they've been stealing longer)
run the day to day affairs (it feels
like moon to moon). Our head man is
a doozie, (not his tribe, but what
the job will do to him). But luckily,
the nation's laws mean little; tribal
custom rules (just look at Brooklyn).

Households keep their juju in an
honored place (a wall-safe's best)
and witch-doctors abound (from shrinks
to hair-dressers or OTB, and many
editorials). The kola nut is passed
around religiously (along with hash
and coke and PCP's).

Our young girls do not have to bring
a dowry (daddy's dropped it all on the
reception, right?) and young men always
promise them the sky (which falls on
them with regularity).

We do make war on other villages (es-
pecially Albany and Staten Island).
Still, the biggest difference is we
need a cutlass both at home and travel-
ling (we only push disarmament abroad).

Oh yes, the natives there are just like
here. They're very nice.

Chorus:

And every day's a market day
(and every day's a gas),
we share a common way of life
(we'd all prefer to pass).

SOUNDINGS

Electric down again. The silence waits
till generators strangle on their black spit,
fans go rigid, people fade through gates
at darkened houses. Nature sense it.
Beetles muffle their weighted wings;
geckos, cruciform, tiptoe down the wall.
Now is its time. Like tombs that shut in kings—
a silence, dominating, occupying all.

At first I am intent, a novice at
its art. I try to fill it with my thoughts
on silence, draw contours on its flat
design, go through the usual oughts,
find something noble to compare it to,
secretly shout it down. What idle zeal.
It comes to me that silences will do,
that unfed hungers also make us real.

CAUSERIE

I tell him things aren't done
like that. (o-*kay*) The system
calls for certain steps, and
(*o*-kay) he has skipped them
all. If only he had gotten to
me sooner (*o*-kay, octave drop
at least), we'd be on top of
things. (o-*kay*, adagio) Now,
could he check the information
he received (*o-kay*, mezzo
piano), see if everything is
there? (o-*kay*, o-*kay*, ru-
bato) Then we press them to
come through on their end
(*o*-kay, almost panic), making
our position unassailable
(*o-kay*, ritardando).

Aieee! I cannot shake its noise.
It doesn't seem to function as
a question, rarely indicates
assent, holds out no promise
nor rejects, does not mark time
or punctuate, describes no state
or quality that's relevant. What
is it?

In former times I'd say he stole
it from my tent, then passed it
through his juju to protect him
from my whims. But now I fear
he uses it to tweak my white
conceit, does funny imitations
of my piping logic. Like as not,

it's more than these. For,
language has a skin, a soil and
foliage with native properties.
Its shoots are difficult to lift,
transport and root again.

Okay. We each come from a diff-
erent chaos. Seven days is not a
schedule for all to keep, nor can
each genesis be put in words. A
stutter doesn't mean we are a
prophet nor does eloquence make
us wise. Why not admit we measure
mystery with different spears?

THIS HAPPENED

Lepers, mostly women, steel-
wool hair neglected, not
much left of limb or time
for that matter, drag
across the foul floor with
dignity, almost ease, to climb
their cot, their kingdom,
neighbored by other kingdoms.
Skin patches like soiled rime
serve as escutcheons,
rank the stage of their disease.
The tinny churchbells chime
toward the distant sheds that
house in their maculated walls,
in the festering grime,
the killer bacilli. On crutches,
barrows, makeshift tripods,
moving to a spastic ragtime
beat, the healthy lepers labor
massward, trundle over the
barely hardened slime,
like the roads at Ypres.
Those in cots cradle cruci-
fixes rubbed to a vintage dime
like their own smooth stumps,
cross themselves best they can,
a fairly efficient mime
of former gestures. No
thought of explanations,
of what unthinking crime
they might have done or
what god would attack them

with such fury. I'm
struck they seem beyond self-
consciousness. They wait
alertly for the paradigm
of Jesus in his suffering and
victory to unfold like a
well-worn nursery rhyme
they once were told.

Then, how they gyrate in their
cots, shoulders working, shake
their bean-clad calabashes,
whoop their toothless allelulias,
hihi hihi hihi hihi hihi!
Visions dance beneath eyelashes
draped in ecstacy, careless
of the world. Cascading,
rhythmic music clashes
with the movement of disjointed
arms conducting it like broken
batons. When holy water splashes
on them, tingles memory and parched
skin, the sound of plucking, thump-
ing escalates. The evil spirit dashes
from the room, tone-deaf, afraid
now of the leprosy it caused,
in this strange heaven gnashes
its teeth, while the lepers feed.

SCHOOL BREAK

Breathless children churn
the red earth to puffs of
rose dust, spectral kites
ascending in their excited
train. Emphatic footballs
arc above the roofs, ignore
the kites. The piping voices
rise, entwine, attempt to
drown the martial drums
that duller spirits practice
on. Too soon the sun
will flay the corrugated tin
above their benches, turn
their eyeballs slate. Thus
certitude retracts its neck
in learning's presence, dreams
of school breaks.

WHEREABOUTS

Bury people in the living
room? Under their favorite
bed? By their window sill watching
hydrangeas and Pride
of Barbados spilling
from the compound wall,
red roofs, sunstruck, stretching
beyond?

I wouldn't like it—
listening to indifferent talk
above my head, hearing market
chatter, the price of thyme,
snatches from the BBC, hit
tunes from a decade hence—
no, not one bit,
if I were consulted.

Have someone, once a year,
think where they planted me?
Even should they shed a tear,
pray for my memory, I'd
be uncomfortable. From here
to there is too delicately vast.
Or is it that I fear
intimacy still?

Hardest would be to
live their ongoing lives
with them, pretend the few
scenarios available to us
are all that new.
And if they blame outcomes
on me—what I failed to do—
do I protest?

Let me rather range
unfriended a while, tasting
what I am. It may be dang-
er quickens the dead,
or at least strange
resting places cushion
parting more, change
overworked horizons.

Will not angels reckon
me anyway, divine my bones,
with exquisite grace beckon
me above? It does not matter
where I lie, a speck on
endless saharas. Only
let me rest my neck on
his in Avalon.

MODESTY

Where is home? My protest's thin.
I say it's any place I'm in,
that I bend with circumstance,
have nerves for every game of chance,
am content with rain or sun
and get along with anyone.

Truth to tell, this sweating sky
depresses me. I like the high
blue of the north that flies away
from you, not rheumy clouds, gray,
crowding in. And there's a time
for flowers not to grow, lime-
colored fall days, woodbine slack
on trees, cold wind. I'd welcome back
winter's plunge (instead of these
unending sprays ravished by bees),
frozen capes on evergreens,
the tarpaulin on plows that means
no more planting, fence posts caked
solid in ice, windows flaked
silk-screen white, a sky inlaid
with winking gemstones made
brighter by the angry glow
of wolves' eyes staring at the snow.

Language is a constant tease,
like tent flaps half open. These
three-tiered tongues begin to pall
when I can't say myself at all.

Made-up words with gaping holes—
I'm left in unintended roles,
stammering. Nor can I scan
the swift text my ear pursues, an
overrun that buries me
in useless scrip. I long to be
where I can hear each word, as far
as whispers in a crowded bar,
understand each curling phrase
without a string to track the maze.

Jesus Lordy God, I o-
verdose on church, am so
wired I light up candles, got
this monkey-angel on me, not
big-time coke but religion, main-
lined, high percentage uncut pain
mixed with grovelling desire
(the dervish dancing on the fire),
guilt, and yet a touchiness
that never gets enough redress.
Street price for its promises
is anything the man says:
rosary laps, novenas, clouds
of flyblown incense, gory shrouds,
chartered trips to some garish shrine,
a broken record—the thin whine
rising from bottomless needs.
Checkmarks against uneven deeds.

Read it in the sacred scrawl,
the curse we cling to after all:

hating Death—what it might bring—
yet envying its famous sting.

Piety is not for me.
I like my God more neighborly,
chatting through the well-kept hedge
of our relationship, no pledge
called for really, casual
about details or schedule,
unclogged access when it counts,
respect in generous amounts,
not a suffocating tie
but friendship with a clear eye,
deepening through interests shared,
not bound just that the other cared.

Wearily, I chew one thing:
I came and leave a hireling.

About the Author—

George McCauley has two previous books of poetry published by Something More (*No Bright Shield* and *Night Air Dancing*). A Jesuit priest, he is currently composing original musical backgrounds for readings of his poetry. The notation for the music in this book was drawn by his collaborator, John Colaiacovo. Tapes of the readings (over music) and of the music itself are available from Something More, 2504 Belmont Ave., Bronx, N.Y. 10458. Tel.: (212) 367-2780